The Dandelion

This book has been reviewed
for accuracy by

Robert L. Costello, Ph.D.
Professor of Biology
University of Wisconsin—Milwaukee

Copyright © 1979, Raintree Publishers Limited

Library of Congress Number: 78-21155

3

Printed in the United States of America.

Library of Congress Cataloging in Publication Data

Hogan, Paula Z
  The dandelion.

  Cover title: The life cycle of the dandelion.
  SUMMARY: Describes in simple terms the life cycle
of the dandelion.
  1. Dandelions — Juvenile literature. [1. Dandelions]
I. Miyake, Yoshi. II. Title. III. Title: The life
cycle of the dandelion.
QK495.C74H63 583'.55 78-21155
ISBN 0-8172-1250-7 lib. bdg.

The

DANDELION

By Paula Z. Hogan

Illustrations by Yoshi Miyake

RAINTREE CHILDRENS BOOKS
Milwaukee • Toronto • Melbourne • London

 # The Dandelion

Dandelions grow in fields and lawns. They grow best in sunny places. The flowers open in the morning. They shut for the night in the late afternoon.

The dandelion looks like one
flower. It is really many small
flowers close together. Each
small flower seems to have only
one petal.

Butterflies and bees fly to
dandelions. They eat the sweet
food inside.

Within every flower a seed can grow. Seeds form where the stem meets the flowers.

After the seeds begin to grow,
the dandelion closes. Petals dry
up and drop to the ground.

After two weeks a seed head opens. Each fruit has a seed. Fine hairs grow from every fruit. When the wind blows, the hairs carry seeds away.

16

Seeds may land on water or
rocks. Dandelions cannot grow in
these places. Sometimes animals
eat the seeds.

The seeds can grow when they
land on the ground. The hairs
fall off. Seed hooks help hold the
seed in the soil.

The seed sends out a shoot. At its tip are the first leaves. In a few days, more leaves will grow.

The new flowering heads are
closed. They open a little more
each day.

Under the ground is a long root. Shorter roots branch out. They draw food and water from the soil. Roots also hold the plant in place.

In winter, the leaves and
flowers die. The roots still live. In
spring, new roots and dandelions
grow from the old roots.

Every plant has many roots and
seeds. No wonder there are so
many dandelions.

Dandelions, thistles, and daisies are in the sunflower family. All have tiny flowers close together.

thistle

daisy

sunflower

GLOSSARY

These words are explained the way they are used in this book. Words of more than one syllable are in parentheses. The heavy type shows which syllable is stressed.

daisy (dai·sy) — a plant that has flowers with many petals. Daisy means "day's eye."

fruit — the part of a dandelion seed-head that holds the seeds

petal (pet·al) one piece of the part of a flower that is brightly colored

root — the part of a plant that is under the ground. The root holds a plant up and also takes food and water from the ground.

seed head (seed·head) — the part of a dandelion that contains the fruit and all the seeds

seed hook (seed·hook) one of the small hooks on the bottom of a dandelion seed that helps hold the seed on the ground

stem — the part of a plant between the root and the flower

sunflower (sun·flow·er) — a tall plant with large flowers